Customer Service

=

Customer Sales

CS=CS

Published in Winter Haven, Florida. Published by Horton International Ministries, Inc.

All inquiries should be addressed to:

Horton International Ministries email:

hortoninternationalminstries@gmail.com

Print 1 – November, 2020

Faye Saxon Horton

Foreword

Good customer experience and service is now a default expectation of a buyer influenced by always being on self- service platforms such as Amazon and Uber.

We are 'never' going back to the old world and now is the time for every member of your team, not only those in a sales role, to appreciate that we all influence a customer's experience of service.

Heed well Faye's words here; for ignorance of the need for service is no excuse to the customer.

Ian Moyse, Sales Leadership & Cloud Computing Thought Leader and Influencer

CS=CS

Introduction

Is there a difference between customer service and customer sales? The customer isn't always right. However, the customer is the customer.

The sales training you received says start to close from the beginning with qualifying statements and questions. Learn up front if this will be a customer and guide the prospect to the outcome you are expecting for both of you.

This sales process is Customer Service. No matter what the product or service you are selling, it will require Customer Service throughout the entire process. Customer Service is required to get the appointment. Customer Service is required to gain the trust of the individual. Customer Service is necessary to discover and meet the needs of the individual. Customer service is required to close the deal. And, customer service is required as follow up to

Faye Saxon Horton

maintain the relationship, grow this customer into an advocate for referrals and keep the customer year after year.

In this book you will learn some basics that you may or may not use currently. These basic steps of Customer Service will help you to hone your Customer Service skills and create more Customer Sales.

Chapter 1

Why?

In 2020, 85% of customer service interactions were automated. In a technological era this has become the norm. However, improving the customer experience is a key factor to ensure customers are satisfied. Satisfied customers mean retention and subsequent sales. Note: Increasing retention by 5% will increase profits by 25-95%.

Customers still care about price and quality. They place an increasing emphasis on customer experience. Customers want to focus on who will take care of their needs and provide value beyond the initial purchase.

According to American Express, 90% of consumers use Customer Service as a factor in buying decisions. 49% of consumers switched companies in 2019 due to poor Customer Service.

Recent statistics show that 73% of customers fall in love and remain loyal to certain brands because of friendly Customer Service. 17% of consumers will spend more for great Customer Service.

Customers who like the Customer Service experience will refer other customers 77% of the time and 93% of those will make repeat purchases.

Customer Service strengthens your brand. It increases your presence and improves customer loyalty. Not to mention that good Customer Service reduces turnover of customers and employees or associates. Sales are boosted by stellar Customer Service which means revenues go right to the bottom line.

Personalized service is fast becoming a dinosaur with automated interactions. Technology has revolutionized a new way of communicating and these new methods can be used to improve Customer Service effectiveness.

Faye Saxon Horton

You will see in this book there are many companies who have built their businesses on good Customer Service. Why? For all the reasons listed above AND because your business can grow with a focus on Customer Service because Customer Service = Customer Sales!

Create and take your Mission Statement with you daily.

Faye Saxon Horton

Chapter 2

Mindset

Well, where do we start? We may as well start at the very beginning. Start with **<u>mindset.</u>** Customer Service isn't a department. Customer service is the concept used throughout your interactions with each individual that you wish to sell a product or service.

Make Customer Service an integral part of your business, starting with the Mission Statement and Vision for your business. It is important to have some concrete idea of what you want your customer expectation of your services or product to be. This means creating for yourself or your company/your brand a Mission Statement that encompasses how Customer Service will be demonstrated.

It does not matter if you are in a company of two employees, 20 employees, 2,000 employees or multi-sectional divisions of an international company that services millions, like Amazon or WalMart, customer service resides in each person who comes in contact with an individual who makes a purchase.

Even if you are a solo entrepreneur who is growing a legacy for the future of you and your family, Customer Service is the backbone of your business. Every successful business has a Mission Statement.

Faye Saxon Horton

Your Mission Statement isn't a plaque on the wall.   The Mission Statement is one that should be carried with you every day. Your Mission Statement should say what you do, who you serve and what differentiates you from others who do the same thing.

This is my personal mission statement. I repeat this during my daily morning affirmations.

"I am good at what I do. Today I will help each person I contact to discover their purpose and live to their potential."

If you are working as an employee, do you know the Mission Statement of your company? Are you able to recite your company's Mission Statement and actually feel your role in the commitment of the statement?

The personal Mission Statement you create is one that you are able to repeat daily as a part of your routine of preparation for business.

Faye Saxon Horton

The Customer is the Customer is the Sale!

Chapter 3

Mission Statement

The three important components to your Mission Statement are listed below.

1. What are you committed to do?

2. Who is your target audience?

3. How will you do this differently from others who do the same thing?

Your Mission Statement must be one that you believe in completely. Mission Statements can be changed as business interest and the direction of your business changes. However, it is important to have a Mission Statement as a guide for what you do, why you do it and for whom you service.

Some examples follow these worksheets to get some ideas about Mission Statements for individuals. These can also be adapted for companies and teams, as well.

Use the worksheets to develop your Mission Statement.

1. What are you committed to do?

2. Who is your target audience?

3. How will you do this differently from others who do the same thing?

EXAMPLES

I bring value to everyone I work with by offering the highest quality products and service.

My mission is to help as many people with the products I offer by giving genuine value and attention to each customer.

I will deliver the best products available to me to my customer.

My mission is to discover the need and fulfill the solution without compromise.

I believe customer engagement is customer satisfaction and customer satisfaction is customer engagement.

My mission is to work hard for you!

Faye Saxon Horton

Every great, well known company has a phenomenal mission statement. Some of them you may recognize. These Mission Statements set the tone for customer engagement.

Let's look at some well-known companies and their Mission Statements to see the relationship of their success to the customer and the commitment made in the Mission Statement.

AMERICAN EXPRESS - *"We work hard every day to make American Express the world's most respected service brand. "*

It is clear what American Express does and how important it is to the brand.

WARBY PARKER – *"To offer designer eyewear at a revolutionary price, while leading the way for socially conscious businesses."*

Warby Parker was founded on the principles that eyeglasses were too expensive. One of the founder's was without glasses for a semester at college because the glasses were too expensive to replace. This led to a revolutionary way of delivering eyeglasses to many people at lower prices.

To further the company's commitment to their customer, Warby Parker gives a pair of glasses to a non-profit organization for every pair that is purchased. Their website has this statement, *"There's nothing complicated about it. Good eyewear, good outcome."*

Faye Saxon Horton

HONEST TEA – *"To create and promote great-tasting, healthy, organic beverages."*

Honest Tea is a wholly owned subsidiary of Coca-Cola Company who started in 1998 and promises to use the best ingredients to bring the best flavored and best quality drinks to the consumer.

IKEA – *"To create a better everyday life for the many people."*

IKEA is a multinational group of Swedish companies headquartered in Delft, Netherlands, that designs and sells ready-to-assemble furniture, kitchen appliances and home accessories, among other useful goods and occasionally home services. Wikipedia. An interesting piece of information about IKEA is that the first telephone number the company lists is Customer Service, not sales. This is a clue to what the company feels is important.

CS=CS

AMAZON – *"**Our mission is to continually raise the bar of the customer experience by using the internet and technology to help consumers find, discover and buy anything, and empower businesses and content creators to maximize their success. We aim to be Earth's most customer centric company.**"*

Amazon's Mission Statement does identify a market but reflects that the concern is for the customer experience.

NORDSTROM – *"To give customers the most compelling shopping experience possible."*

You may have heard the famous Nordstrom Customer Service Story. This is real. Nordstrom's started in 1901 as a shoe store and grew to become a full line retailer of clothes, shoes, jewelry, and accessories.

In 1975 a gentleman walked into a Nordstrom's store to return four automobile tires. He purchased the tires from a store that previously was located where the now

Nordstrom's store stood. Yes, I know you are thinking. Nordstrom's doesn't sell tires. So, he was just out of luck.

Not so fast. After explaining his situation to a store clerk not only was the gentleman able to the tires (left them at Nordstrom's even though the store did not sell tires), Nordstrom's refunded his full purchase price. Now that's Customer Service. This story has lasted for years and has created for Nordstrom's the ultimate in Customer Service.

'Our commitment is 100% to customer service. We are not committed to financial markets, we are not committed to real estate markets, we are not committed to a certain amount of profit. We are only committed to customer service. If we make a profit, that's great. But customer service is first. If I'm a salesperson on the floor and I know that the people who own this place are committed to customer service, then I am free to find new ways to give great customer service. I know that I won't be criticized for taking care of a customer. I will only be criticized if I don't take care of a customer."

— John Nordstrom

CS=CS

Business is about identifying a prospect's needs and offering Customer Service solutions that create Customer Sales.

Faye Saxon Horton

Chapter 4

Customer's Needs

Creating the proper mindset to deliver great Customer Service is the number one key to Customer Service = Customer Sales. The other keys I do not plan to identify by number as they are all important.

Evaluate each element of Customer Service in this book and determine which ones you do well and which ones you may not do so well. Work on the ones you are not using to master them, while continuing to work with the ones you are using well.

Respect is at the very top of the list. I mention it now as you must respect yourself to respect others. Not all customers will be pleasant customers. You may never know why a person feels or answers the way that they do. Perhaps they are having a bad day or perhaps they have had an awful existence (real or fabricated).

You never know what roads this person travelled to get to you. Be patient. Be respectful. Always use eye contact. And most of all LISTEN. LISTEN to what the person is saying. Become an expert at asking questions that will give you the basic reasons the purchase is necessary. Yes, often an individual will not realize a purchase is necessary. The purchase of goods or services from

Faye Saxon Horton

you may be a dream purchase, a wish they have had for a long time.

In life insurance, as an example, I am not thinking people wake up in the morning to say, today I am going to buy life insurance. However, there are many mornings that same person will wake and say I need to get my life insurance in order. This might be something that has been on their minds for some time, however, they just haven't taken the action to do anything about it.

Respect includes addressing the person by their **name.** If you are unable to pronounce the name correctly, ask the person to help you. Certain dialects and pronunciations may not be as you think. Simply explain you are not sure and would not want to mispronounce the name. "Would you tell me how I should pronounce your name, please?" **Note: Please and thank you continue to be an extremely great way to be respectful.**

CS=CS

A name is important. Once you get that name and you are pronouncing the name correctly, you can bring the prospect's attention back to your conversation simply by repeating their name. Learn quickly how the customer wants to be addressed and use that address frequently throughout your conversation.

Notice I said "conversation" not "presentation". This brings me to the next point of respect. Be as conversational as possible. It is often said we have two ears and one mouth for a reason. LISTEN.

Listening becomes an art, just as conversation rather than presentation. You listen not only for the things you want to hear but for those subtle things you were not expecting to hear. This is critical to identifying the prospect's need.

Faye Saxon Horton

There will be some things about your product or service that you must give to the prospect, however, to move this prospect to a customer you must meet their need. Don't assume you know the need even though the telltale signs are so evident that you can generalize what their economic status may be, what the need may be and what their budget may be. Sometimes you may generalize the level of understanding the customer may have about the product or service you offer. Throw this out with the dishwater. Use a proven system of qualifying questions to learn what needs the customer may have.

The questions listed here are applicable to any conversation, no matter the product or service you offer. Whether I am meeting a Medicare customer or a life insurance prospect my questions start in the same fashion. Now, depending on how the customer receives me and the formality of the conversation, I will ask these questions differently to each prospect. However, they are the same basic questions.

1.   What do you have now?

This question is to learn the starting point of my discovery. This one question alone may not give all the answers. It may take a few other questions to get the real answer with all the details. This is a good starting question no matter what product or service you are selling. Some examples where this question works well:

Faye Saxon Horton

a. Selling appliances – what type, make, model does the customer have now or are they replacing a particular appliance or acquiring for the first time?

b. Selling Cars – What type car do they have now, how long have they had it? Is this a first car? What cars are in the family? With which cars are they most comfortable?

c. Selling Financial Services – Do they have investments now? Any Life insurance in place? Any pensions or other income? Any 401K with or without employer matches?

d. Selling digital services – What do you have in place, i.e. website, landing pages, payment portals? Who administers those? How are they managed?

Faye Saxon Horton

2.   What do you like about what you have now? What works well. What are the parts that you would not want to give up? Where would you put what you have now on a scale of 1 to 5 with 5 being the best—top of the line?

3.   What would you like to see different? What would you change if you could make your own product/service? What would you want to see that will make your life better? What would help you conduct business more efficiently?

4.   Do you make the decisions about purchases or is there a committee or someone else who will help with decision making?

5.   Summarize what the prospect has told you. Repeat by the answers to the prospect using the words given to you. This solidifies the information in their minds, as their own words.

CS=CS

"He profits most who serves best."

Arthur F. Sheldon

Faye Saxon Horton

Chapter 5

Sales

Your expectation is a sale. The customer's expectation is that their needs will be met. Once you have established the need and matched the proper product/service to that need you are on the road to having both your expectations met.

The sale is all about the prospect's feelings and emotions. Have you garnered enough information from them that you can now repeat back the need, in their words, so that the prospect realizes the buying decision is theirs and they are NOT being sold?

Customer Service continues with providing so much value to the prospect that they are:

- ✓ Ready to buy
- ✓ Ready to refer you to others
- ✓ Ready to trust you for future sales
- ✓ Ready to become your advocate

Close the deal with the customer knowing and accepting the value you have brought to their lives. Have you carried out your Mission Statement with this customer?

Make this a memorable experience for the customer. Let the customer know the process for completing your application. Be certain the customer is aware what they have purchased, when they might expect more communications from you and your company, and what those communications will be.

Provide Customer Service to the very end. Review what has been said. Review the next steps. Leave the customer in anticipation of what happens next. If you have provided good Customer Service you have a sale.

Ask for the referral. Imagine if for each customer you meet you get a referral? Do what you do so well that the customer will want to see it again and again and send their friends to hear the same story. Exceed the customer's expectations every time.

CS=CS

Chapter 6

Checklist

Let's close with a checklist of the actions you can take that will ensure great Customer Service.

1. Look the part. Professionally dressed.
2. Be kind and courteous.
3. Address the customer politely and respectfully by name.
4. Be considerate of the customer's time. Always arrive on time or call if you are not on time.
5. Ask questions and receive answers discreetly.
6. Be aware of the tone used when speaking.
7. Smile.
8. Laugh with the customer.
9. Be serious yet kind.
10. Ask the hard questions in an easy manner.
11. Deliver more than the customer expects.
12. Only tell what you know to be factual.
13. Provide solutions to the customer's needs.
14. Identify the customer's need.
15. Listen intently.
16. Speak at a pace the customer will understand.
17. Use correct terms to describe the product/service.
18. Be complementary, but honest.

CS=CS

19. Show the customer that you care about their needs.
20. Use real life stories to illustrate a point.
21. Take good notes.
22. Remember the pet's name.
23. Greet with a smile and leave with a smile.
24. Ask for referrals in more than one way.
25. Consider when your next touch will be and let the customer know to expect it.
26. Send a thank you note.
27. Add the customer to your CRM or database with the notes you have taken.
28. Record the customer's birth date for birthday cards.
29. Note any unusual things that the customer may have, i.e. grows orchids as a hobby.
30. Be comfortable and make your customer comfortable.
31. Talk to the customer rather than present to the customer. Conversation vs. Presentation.
32. Show a genuine interest. If you have no genuine interest, as an example, in pets don't fake it.

Faye Saxon Horton

33. From the beginning get the "name" right.
34. Cross all your "t's" and dot all your "I's".
35. Should you forget something let the customer know right away.
36. Follow up as you said you would.
37. Deliver more than expected.
38. Use words that will be familiar to your customer.
39. Never talk down to anyone.
40. Know your product before the customer meeting.
41. Use positive sentences and words.
42. Control the conversation.
43. Listen, but refocus when necessary.
44. Set high standards for yourself.
45. Remember your Mission Statement.
46. Don't rush the conversation, but stay focused.
47. Help the customer to help themselves.
48. Give enough supporting information to make a point but not drown the thought.
49. Please and Thank You!
50. Stay human!

Made in the USA
Coppell, TX
24 December 2020

47042306R10026